A Life Well Commentated

The Fascinating Journey of Jim Nantz.

Leslie G. Mika

Copyright Page

All rights reserved. No part of this publication may be reproduced, distributed, or transmitted in any form or by any means, including photocopying, recording, or other electronic or mechanical methods, without the prior written permission of the publisher, except in the case of brief quotations embodied in critical reviews and certain other non-commercial uses permitted by copyright law.

Copyright © (Leslie G. Mika), (2023).

Table of Contents

PROLOGUE 3
Childhood and education 5
Height and weight of Jim 7
Jim's Career in Broadcasting 8
    Prior to CBS Sports 8
    On CBS Sports, ... 8
Jim and his teammate 10
    The NFL airs on CBS 11
A new beginning 13
Appearances in the media 15
Timeline of his Career 17
Honours and awards 19
Dustin Johnson and Nantz 23
The voice of Jim Nantz is replicated on the Dan Patrick program. 25
    Quick sentences in the manner of Jim Nantz 25
Income, Annual Salary, and Net Worth 26
Endorsement Agreements 27
Jim Nantz Quotations 28

PROLOGUE

James William Nantz III is an American sportscaster who has worked on telecasts of the National Football League (NFL), NCAA Division I, the NBA, and the PGA Tour since the 1980s.

Jim Nantz was born on May 17, 1959, in Charlotte, North Carolina. Nantz has hosted CBS Sports' coverage of the Masters Tournament since 1989. Later that year, he was hired as the play-by-play announcer for CBS's premier NFL game.

In May 2008, he published his first book, "Always by My Side - A Father's Grace, and Also Sports Journey Unlike Any Other." Furthermore, Nantz debuted his private wine label, "The Calling," with its first vintage released in 2012.

Many sports fans and aficionados across the world recognize Jim Nantz's voice. He is a well-known sporting figure. In 2023, the sportscaster will call his final NCAA Tournament 'Final Four' before being replaced by Ian Eagle.

Childhood and education

"Hello, friends," says Nantz at the start of each of his broadcasts. The greeting arose as a method for Nantz to identify himself to his father, who had Alzheimer's disease.

Jim Nantz was born on May 17, 1959, in Charlotte, North Carolina, as James William Nantz III. He grew raised in New Orleans, Louisiana, Colts Neck Township, New Jersey, and Marlboro Township, New Jersey. He attended Marlboro High School in Marlboro.

He was a well-known athlete in high school, serving as co-captain and number-one player for the basketball team. He was also a member of the Bamm Hollow Country Club and a co-captain of the golf team.

Nantz then moved to Texas to attend the University of Houston. He was a member of the University of Houston's men's golf team.

He shared a dorm with Fred Couples and Blaine McAllister, both of whom went on to play professional golf.

He majored in broadcasting and graduated with a Bachelor of Arts in Radio and Television Broadcasting in 1981. It was during this time at the university that Nantz got his first experience in sports broadcasting with the CBS Radio Network by transmitting taped interviews to Win Elliot for Elliot's Sports Central USA weekend reports.

Height and weight of Jim

Nantz is presently 63 years old and celebrates his birthday every year on May 17th. Taurus is his astrological sign. The sportscaster was a standout athlete in high school and at the University of Houston. This explains his incredible athletic body, as well as his round-off height and weight.

He stands 6 feet 3 inches (1.90 meters) tall and weighs around 75 kg (165 pounds). His hair has a deep brownish tone.

Jim's Career in Broadcasting

Before CBS Sports

In the early 1980s, Nantz began working as a sportscaster and anchor for KHOU Houston, a CBS-affiliated television station licensed to Houston, Texas.

From 1982 until 1985, he served as a weekend sports anchor for KSL-TV, an NBC-affiliated television station in Salt Lake City, Utah.

Nantz and Hot Rod Hundley worked for KSL-TV, where they called BYU football and Utah Jazz basketball games.

On CBS Sports,

After joining CBS Sports in 1985, Nantz began as a studio host for CBS Sports' coverage of college basketball and football events.

He has served as an on-course reporter for the PGA Tour and as a commentator for NFL games on Westwood One. From 1988 through 1990, he called

Saturday Night Football games for CBS Radio Sports, which was still in operation at the time.

Jim and his teammate

James Nantz has been a reporter for CBS Masters Tournament coverage since 1989. He worked alongside Billy Packer from 1991 to 2008, commentating on the NCAA Final Four men's basketball championships. Clark Kellogg was his analyst from 2008 until 2013. During the Final Four from 2010 to 2013, the famed basketball head coach and former NBA player Steve Kerr joined them from Turner Sports.

Greg Anthony then collaborated with Nantz from 2013 to 2014. Greg Anthony was immediately suspended, and his replacements, Bill Raftery and Grant Hill were chosen to work with James Nantz.

Aside from that, he garnered a lot of attention for roasting NFL star Jamaal Charles, who cost his team a win following a fumble.

The NFL airs on CBS

Jim Nantz presented The NFL Today on CBS from 1998 to 2003, which was the NFL's pre-game show. Following that, in 2004, he was promoted to the lead play-by-play commentator for The NFL on CBS.

As a result of the adjustment, Greg Gumbel was sent to the studio, while Jim Nantz was assigned to the stadium booth with Phil Simms.

In 1991 and 1992, Nantz collaborated on NFL broadcasts alongside commentator Hank Stram. Then, in 1993, while Greg Gumbel was covering the American League Championship for CBS, Nantz temporarily filled in for him.

CBS's second-round playoff game between Dallas and Green Bay was called by Jim Nantz and Randy Cross. Nantz was in charge of the play-by-play for Super Bowl XLII. On the 4th of February, 2007. He joined the ranks of Curt Gowdy, Kevin Harlan, and Dick Enberg as the only play-by-play announcers to broadcast both a Super Bowl and an NCAA Men's Basketball Championship Game.

James is one of only two men to have hosted a Super Bowl, announced an NCAA Men's Basketball Championship game, and hosted The Masters from Butler Cabin. Both of these sportscasters accomplished this accomplishment while working for CBS.

In 2014, Jim Nantz and his broadcast partner Phil Simms called Thursday Night Football games for CBS and NFL Network, with Tracy Wolfson serving as the sideline reporter for the Thursday and Sunday games on CBS.

Nantz and Romo revealed that Super Bowl LIII would be held in 2019 and Super Bowl LV will be held in 2021. Following that, Tony Romo, the former Dallas Cowboys quarterback, took over as colour commentator for CBS' NFL telecasts, replacing Phil Simms.

A new beginning

Sandy Montag, Nantz's long-time agent, revealed that the veteran play-by-play broadcaster has renewed his contract with the network, where he works as a main voice on everything from the NFL and NCAA men's basketball tournament to the Masters and PGA Tour.

Nantz will call his second Super Bowl alongside Tony Romo and sixth overall in February 2021. Since 1991, Nantz has been the host of March Madness.

Furthermore, Tony Romo, who has worked with Jim Nantz and has been praised for his ability to predict which plays teams will run, got a deal with CBS in 2020 at $17.5 million per year, which is likely the highest sports analyst contract in television history.

Nantz's contract with CBS was set to end in early 2021, but he agreed to a new deal with the network. According to several accounts, his annual pay might reach $10.5 million.

Following the extension of his current contract, he plans to become the first CBS broadcaster to call 50 Masters Tournaments. He would accomplish this achievement by the age of 75 in 2035.

Appearances in the media

Jim has been on The Price is Right to give a CBS Sports Showcase prize including CBS Sports assets. Nantz appeared as himself in the 1996 film Tin Cup.

He has appeared in episodes of various TV shows, including Arliss, Yes, Dear, Criminal Minds, and How I Met Your Mother. In the short-lived Clubhouse series, Nantz acted as an announcer for a fictional baseball club. Scrapple, a 1998 film, featured his voice.

Since 2009, Nantz has also served as a guest commentator for the BBC's final round of the Open Championship. Jim Nantz and Garry McCord collaborated on the 1999 golf game Jack Nicklaus 6: Golden Bear Challenge, which was released for extended remarks.

Jim also recorded for his commentary that was featured in the Golden Tee Golf arcade game series. From 2012 to 2016, Nantz and Phil Simms were the commentators for the popular Madden NFL franchise, until being replaced by Brandon Gaudin and Charles Davis.

In 2013, Nantz appeared in an advertisement for Papa John's Pizza alongside former Denver Broncos quarterback Peyton Manning and Papa John's Pizza founder John Schnatter.

Timeline of his Career

- NCAA Football on CBS - studio host, 1985-1988
- 1986-present: PGA Tour on CBS (host since 1994)
- College Basketball on CBS from 1986 through 1990 - studio host
- NBA on CBS from 1986 to 1989 - main play-by-play
- From 1987 through 1990, CBS Radio broadcast NFL play-by-play.
- Play-by-play coverage of the US Open (tennis) from 1987 through 1995
- The Masters has been held every year since 1989.
- NCAA Football on CBS, 1989-1991; 1996-1997 - lead play-by-play
- College Basketball on CBS/Turner from 1990 through 2023 - lead play-by-play
- 1988-1993; 2004-present: NFL on CBS - play-by-play (1993 as second; 2004 as first)

- Weekend daytime co-host for the Winter Olympics in 1992 and 1994.
- Macy's Thanksgiving Day Parade host (under the title "The Thanksgiving Day Parade on CBS"), 1994-1995; 2000-2001
- From 1998 to 2003, he was the presenter of NFL Today.
- Olympic Winter Games 1998 - primetime host
- Thursday Night Football (2014-2017) - lead play-by-play

Honours and awards

- Winner of two Sports Emmy Awards for Outstanding Sports Personality, Play-by-Play (in 2009 and 2010).
- National Sports Caster of the Year five times (1998, 2005, 2007, 2008, and 2009), according to the NSMA.
- 2002 The Basketball Hall of Fame's Curt Gowdy Award.
- The Pro Football Hall of Fame presented Pete Rozelle with the Radio-Television Award in 2011.
- 2021 GCSAA the Golf Course Superintendents Association of America's Old Tom Morris Award NSMA Hall of Fame inductee (class of 2021)

Wife, Relationships, and Children

Nantz and his first wife, Ann-Lorraine "Lorrie" Nantz, had a daughter called Caroline and lived in Westport, Connecticut. Ann-Lorraine and James had been married for 26 years until they divorced in 2009.

Following their divorce, the court ordered James to pay Ann-Lorraine $916k per year in child support and alimony. Before the official divorce announcement, James admitted to dating a 29-year-old woman.

Although the judge determined that this particular occurrence had nothing to do with the marriage issues and that Ann-Lorraine and James' relationship had deteriorated years before the extramarital affair.

Jim Nantz then married Courtney in a ceremony at the Pebble Beach Golf Links in Pebble Beach, California.

Their wedding included a celebrity guest list that included Bush, Arnold Palmer, Robert Kraft, and Tom Brady.

Since then, the couple has had two children: a girl named Finely Cathleen Nantzborn, born in 2014, and a son named Jameson Nantz, born in 2016. Aside from that, he and his family live in a nice mansion in Pebble Beach.

Nantz is a foodie who likes his toast burned to a crisp but has never received it while ordering it at a restaurant. As a result, he kept a laminated photo of burnt toast in his wallet to demonstrate how he loved his bread.

"I'm a breakfast guy: three eggs scrambled, with bacon and wheat toast, burnt," Nantz told Golf Digest in 2016. "The problem is that it never returned burned." For years, it would arrive limp and tanned, bringing breakfast to a halt when I returned the bread."

"It was costing me 10 minutes a day, which multiplied by six days a week is four hours a month," Nantz noted. That equates to 48 hours (two full days) every year. My friends, "Money is currency."

"My wife, Courtney, had had enough of hearing me whine about it. She discovered an image of a kitchen toaster ejecting two pieces of burned toast on the Internet. My wife shrunk it, printed it, and laminated it."

"She insisted on me putting it in my wallet. When I place my order, I show my waiter the photo. I get funny glances, but I tell you that the toast is now black and terrifying, exactly the way I like it."

Dustin Johnson and Nantz

Dustin Johnson's victory at the Masters was a dream come true. Dustin Johnson noted for his stoicism, revealed how much he loves the game and is overcome with emotions during an interview with CBS' Amanda Ballionis after Tiger Woods placed the green jacket on him.

"As a kid, I always wanted to be a Masters champion." It's difficult to speak. I've never had such much trouble assembling my thoughts. I'm pretty excellent on the golf course. I'm not out here. "It's difficult to speak," Dustin said.

Dustin became upset to the point that he couldn't finish his idea, prompting Jim Nantz to put the entire incident into context.

"I think that's one of the most incredible things I've ever seen from Dustin Johnson, right there," remarked Nantz.

"You get a lot of individuals who wonder what's going on inside the athletes' heads. It's so simple these days to submit an opinion or a comment on a website or social media. And people feel good about themselves for attempting to bring down these great people who work so hard, as well as the fire that burns inside them. You just noticed it right there. That was simply a reflection of how much it mattered to him and how hard he fought for it."

The voice of Jim Nantz is replicated in the Dan Patrick program.

Nantz has been a long-time Masters commentator and is recognized for his slightly distinct catchphrases, and every year in the run-up to the Masters, Dan Patrick Show hosts a Jim Nantz sound-alike competition.

Jim Nantz is also a frequent guest on the show. In 2018, there was a guy who delivered some lines in the identical Jim Nantz way, complete with the CBS emblem affixed to the chest pocket of his navy blue jacket.

Quick sentences in the manner of Jim Nantz

So, here are some of Jim Nantz's fast phrases: "Ubiquitous nightingale," "Fred Couples has a supple spine," "Clint Eastwood climbs the dogwood," "Is that a gentoo penguin."

Jim Nantz says these lines in real life, just minutes before his live Masters Monologue begins.

Income, Annual Salary, and Net Worth

Nantz has been in the broadcasting industry for a long time and has participated in a variety of shows. According to some accounts, he is paid around $10.5 million per year by CBS.

He used his winnings to renovate his home and build a mini-golf course in his garden. Jim also launched his wine label, however, it is unclear how much money he made from the first vintage release in 2012.

The media personality has a net worth of $15 million as of 2023, which will almost certainly increase given his fame, repute, and popularity.

Endorsement Agreements

Although no information on endorsement arrangements could be found, Jim Nantz is one of the most well-known NFL pundits today.

From college games to Super Bowls, it's difficult to find a sport in which Nantz has not provided commentary. According to reports, he also receives an extra $4 million in postponed remuneration from an agreement with the golf business Titleist.

Jim Nantz is also quite interested in politics. He gave the most money to Jeb Bush's campaign in 2016 and is a close friend of the Bush family. Not only that, but he has given to Joe Lieberman.

Jim Nantz Quotations

"Sometimes when you think you can't, you can," said UCONN's coach, "and UCONN has won the national championship."

Some people claim that the fight between Okafor and Schenscher is the best championship game matchup since Olajuwon and Ewing.

"I'm fortunate to have wonderful friends, and there have been many men in my life who have been more than just friends."

Made in the USA
Columbia, SC
23 May 2025